Be Found On The 1st Page of Google!

Search Engine Optimization to Rank Your Business Online.

SEO Online Marketing with SEO Diva

You do NOT NEED to be Tech Savvy to Dominate Your Niche with SEO.

Copyright © SEO Online Marketing with SEO Diva Be Found On 1st Page of Google. All rights reserved

Table of Content:

Book Description	Page 4
Copyright	Page 5
Why SEO Diva	Page 6
What is SEO	Page 7
How To SEO	Page 8
The 3 Basic SEO Elements	Page 9
Basic Element of SEO – Keywords	Page 10
Basic Element of SEO – Content	Page 11
Basic Element of SEO – Backlinks	Page 12
Why SEO	Page 13
What To SEO	Page 14
SEO Website	Page 15
On-Site SEO	Page 16-18
Off-Site SEO	Page 19-20
SEO Wordpress Theme	Page 21
SEO Plug-ins For Website	Page 22
SEO Tools	Page 23
SEM or Search Engine Marketing	Page 24
SEO Awesome Ranking Your Online Business	Page 25

Copyright © SEO Online Marketing with SEO Diva Be Found On 1st Page of Google. All rights reserved

3 SEO Basic Elements Rules for Your Youtube Channel & Videos	Page 26
Social Media Platforms	Page 27
Compelling Content for Conversion	Page 28
Branding and Conversion	Page 29
Thank You	Page 30
Back Cover	Page 31
About the Author	Page 32

Copyright © SEO Online Marketing with SEO Diva Be Found On 1st Page of Google. All rights reserved

Book Description:

SEO Diva helps businesses rank on first page of Google and Youtube with SEO Awesome Ranking Technique.

This book helps entrepreneurs, "wantepreneurs" and marketers who want to learn and apply SEO (search engine optimization) to help rank their business on Google Search Engine.

Learn and understand the 3 Basic SEO Elements and other essential methods that needs to be applied to get a good quality SEO Website.

Copyright © SEO Online Marketing with SEO Diva Be Found On 1st Page of Google. All rights reserved

Copyright © SEO Online Marketing with SEO Diva Be Found On 1st Page Of Google All rights reserved.

Written by: Judy Toh

Reproduction of the whole or any part of the contents without written permission from the author is prohibited.

For rights or permissions enquiries, contact us at http://dunsayBOJIO.com

ISBN-13: 978-1548637071

ISBN-10: 1548637076

Copyright © SEO Online Marketing with SEO Diva Be Found On 1st Page of Google. All rights reserved

Why SEO Diva?

If you are looking for the best, fastest, easiest and most effective method to rank your business on Google & Youtube, then look for SEO Diva!

We do not fatify the content to get more from you. We give you the basics of what you need to know about SEO.

The best thing is that you do not need to be tech savvy or an IT expert to be able to rank your business on google and youtube with the method shared by SEO Diva!

SEO Secrets Unveiled – The Best SEO Awesome Ranking Technique

So, if simple, fast, easy and effective SEO Method is what you are looking for to rank your business online, then, continue reading!

In this book, SEO Diva will share with you the secrets that can help you rank your business online within an hour or so with the powerful SEO Awesome Ranking Technique.

Yes, read on to unveil the SEO Secrets now and apply them onto your business online!

What is SEO?

SEO stands for Search Engine Optimization. It means how well you optimize your online content or website on search engines like google, yahoo, bing and others.

SEO friendly content can be easily found on search engines when customers look for you online.

Ranking Your Business Online with SEO

For instance, if you sell "an international best selling ebook", you want to make sure your online content can be found by your customers or potential customers when they key in the word "international best selling ebook" or the name of your product and services.

SEO is an organic method that helps your content or website be found online.

There are many elements involved in SEO. However, stay tune as it is not as difficult or complicated as most of the gurus made them to be.

How To SEO?

Yes, the questions many online marketers always ask themselves! How to SEO my content! Well, believe it or not, it simply comprises of 3 main basic elements that you need to do on a consistently manner.

The 3 Basic SEO Elements

And the 3 basic and most important element of SEO are your:

1) Keywords
2) Content
3) Backlinks

Understand and do these 3 basic fundamental for your online business and you will be easily found on the search engines easily.

3 Basic SEO Elements

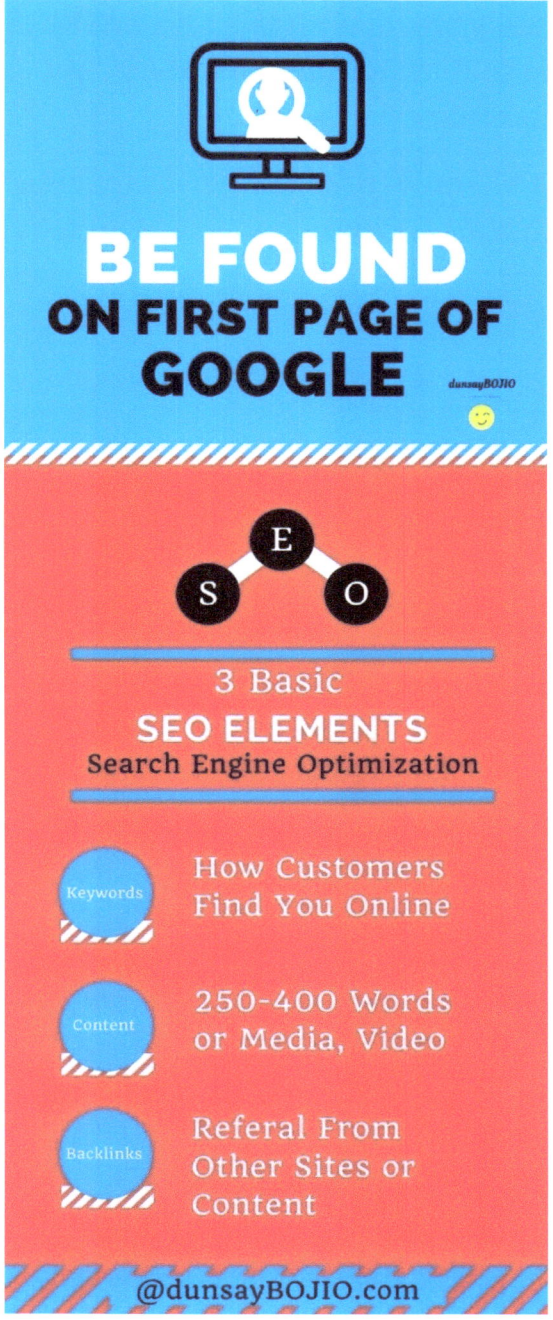

Copyright © SEO Online Marketing with SEO Diva Be Found On 1st Page of Google. All rights reserved

Basic Element of SEO - Keywords

Oh yes! It usually starts with your KEYWORDS! What are the keywords that customers would usually use to find your products and services?

Let's take the example of the "international best selling ebook". For a start, I would go to google search engine to search for the relevant keywords for "international best selling ebook.

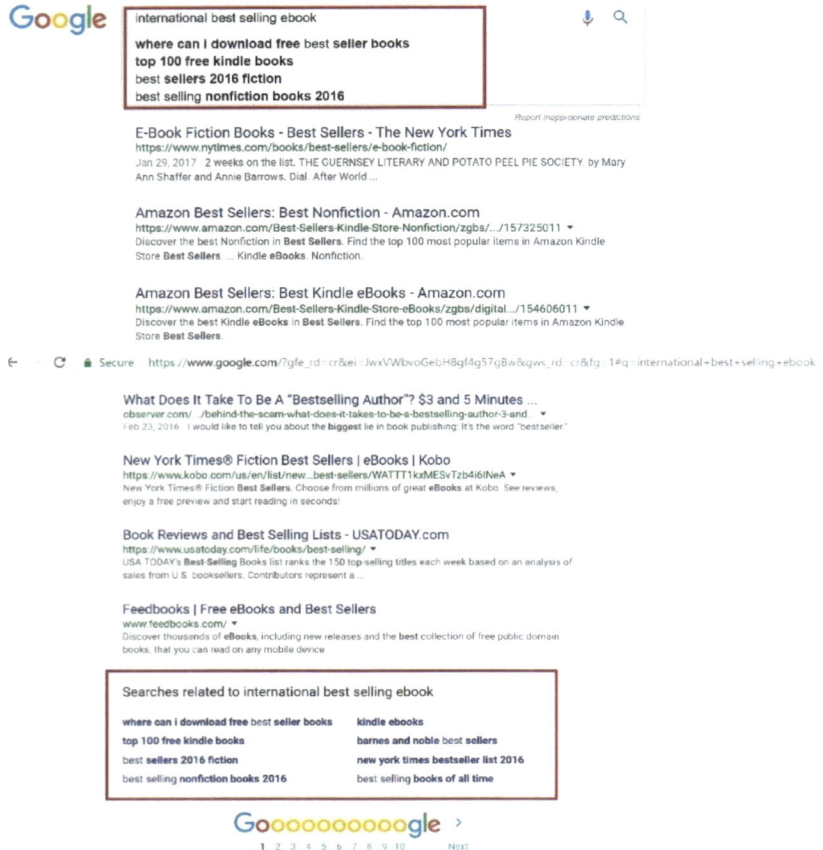

Basic Element of SEO – Content

Once you have done your keywords research for your business, you can start to include these keywords onto your content. Yes, your content is still king!

It is essential to ensure that you do not overstuffed your content with the keywords. Make it pleasant and easy for the consumers and search engines.

Keywords Density In Content

However, having said that you must also ensure that your content has the right density of the keywords relevance.

It is recommended that each piece of content like your article, post or page consists of at least 250-450 words with proper keywords for the title, subtitles.

Saving Your Media with Proper Keywords

Your content can also consist of pictures, make sure each of them are properly saved with the relevant business keywords. Same goes for your video content.

Keyword links from one page or post to another within your own website will also help with your SEO website.

Basic Element of SEO – Backlinks

Backlinks are the JUICE of SEO. Backlinks are similar to online referral from other sites or platforms to your content or website. To search engines, backlinks are how well other relevant sites or businesses other than your own, are referring to your content.

Creating Backlinks

So, if you are going to create your own backlinks for your website or online marketing platforms, it is important to place your backlinks with sites that are similar to your business. The more relevant the sites are the better quality your backlinks are considered by search engines.

Let's take the example of the "international best selling ebook", if your backlinks to your book is coming from places that market or sell books or ebooks, the more relevant and high quality your backlinks are.

So, it is important for you to have links from online book stores or places that sells books to refer to your book, to increase the visibility of your book online.

Backlinks or links back to your content or own site that markets your book can also be placed at relevant book forums, articles related to books and international books.

Why SEO?

SEO is an organic method for you to build your online business. Making your website or online marketing platforms or content SEO friendly is a great long term investment for your online business. When you continue to build and put in relevant contents for your business online, you are building an asset of presence of your business online.

SEO is a Long Term Investment For Your Online Business

That is why many online business owners are spending tons of their marketing budget onto SEO for their online business and visibilities of their online presence.

Be Relevant and Consistent

Updating your website with relevant and most up to date content will help customers understand and stay updated with your offerings and at the same time search engines love them too, helping you rank your business online.

What to SEO?

What do you need to SEO? The ideal method is to ensure that every single piece of your online marketing materials or online content are search engine optimized.

So, how do you do that?

Always be relevant and consistent in your SEO effort for your online business.

Make sure that all your online marketing platforms are SEO friendly, your website, the site structures, your blog, your blog post, your blog page, your facebook page, your youtube channel, your video, the pictures included onto your online platforms.

All these can be made search engine optimized friendly.

SEO Website

It is essential for you to have a search engine optimized website. The structure of your website must be search engine friendly.

So, what are the elements of SEO that search engine look for on each website.

They are basically:

*Title of Your Page/Post

*Meta keywords

*Meta description

*Internal links

*Keyword optimized content or pictures

*H1 to h5 html density

*Xml or txt sitemaps

Wordpress Platform for Your Website

Wordpress platform is SEO friendly and there are many free or premium theme that you can upload to use for your SEO website.

In addition, plug-ins are also some features that can compliment and help with your on-site SEO for your website.

Copyright © SEO Online Marketing with SEO Diva Be Found On 1st Page of Google. All rights reserved

On-site SEO

On-site SEO starts with the SEO friendly structure of your website. Wordpress platform offers SEO friendly structure. Wordpress has many SEO friendly theme that you can choose to create or design your own SEO website.

On-site SEO starts with your URL. Use SEO friendly url like https://dunsayBOJIO.com/On-Site-SEO instead of https://dunsayBOJIO.com/2017-06-28/Online/On-Site-SEO

Title

The closer the keyword is to the beginning of the title the stronger the quality of the SEO.

HTML

Use html h1 wrap on your keyword for each page or post of your article

Use html h2 wrap on other parts of subtitles with the keywords for your article

Media SEO Optimized

Engage with image, video or diagram but remember to also tag them or title them with your keyword for optimization.

Placing of Keywords

Make sure that your keywords are placed in the first sentence of your description or start of the article.

Links

Use internal link from an article to another within your own website.

Use outbound link to preferably authoritative site to help google see the relevance of your site to another website.

Website Speed

Improve the speed of your website by ensuring that you optimize your picture, videos or diagrams.

Long Tail Keywords

Throw in your keywords and long tail keywords in part of your article.

Number of Words In Content

Content of 400 words or more are highly recommended for every article. This will also help reduce the over density of the use of your keywords on the article.

Relevant and Consistent Content

Make sure that your content is relevant and interesting as it increases the time your visitor spend on the page, reducing the bounce rate or how soon before they exit your article or page.

All these makes great on-site SEO for your website or online content.

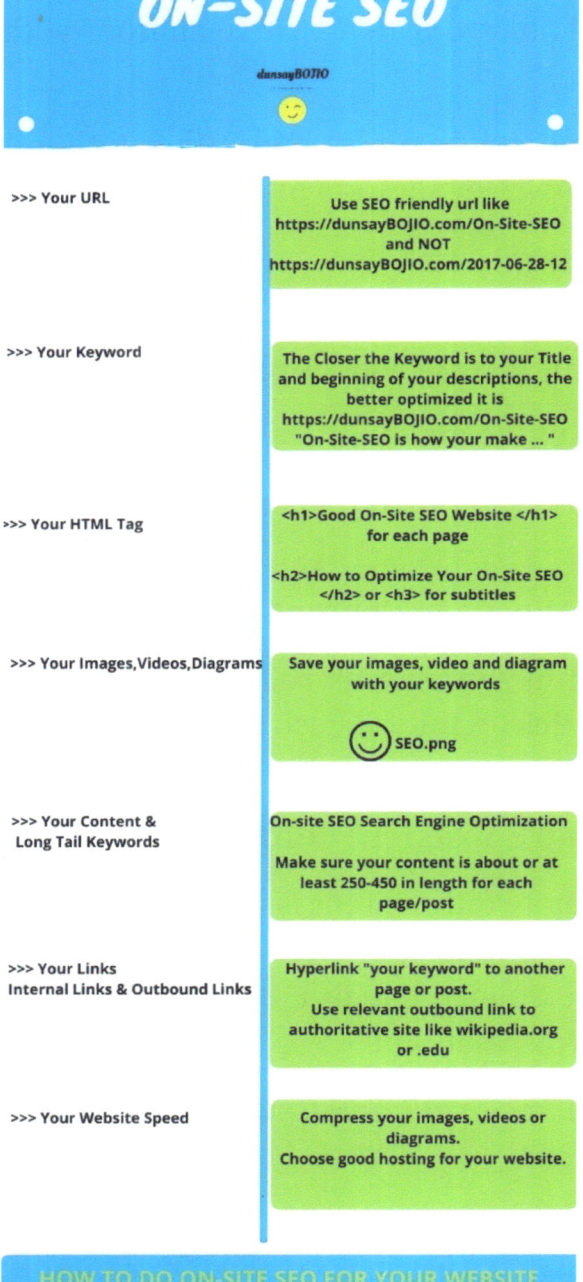

Copyright © SEO Online Marketing with SEO Diva Be Found On 1st Page of Google. All rights reserved

Off-Site SEO

Off-site SEO for website is the works done outside of your website to improve on the search engine optimization of your websites.

Online Referals

The main ones are backlinks where other websites, content, articles, forums are linking back to your website. This means those sites and content are refering your website.

Quality of Off-Site SEO for Website

It is important that the backlinks are relevant to your business, products and services. The more relevant it is the stronger the SEO quality of the backlink is.

As search engines change their algorithm often, we do not know the weightage of the importance of backlinks. However, it is believed that relevant backlinks from sites and other platforms to your site or content helps increase the trustworthiness and popularity of your site. This carries about 50% of your SEO for your website.

The consistency of your content or freshness of your content also helps with your SEO.

The quality of the backlinks consist of how authoritative or high page rank of the site linking in to your site, the relevance of content or topic, the keyword link or anchor text that hyperlinks into your site, the number of other links on the page and how new is the content.

And of course all these must be complimented with good on-site SEO for your website.

SEO Wordpress Theme

There are many wordpress theme template that you can use to create and design your search engine optimized website.

You can add SEO wordpress friendly theme by typing in "seo friendly" in the add theme column.

SEO Plug-ins for Website

SEO Plug-ins can help you improve on your SEO for your website. You can upload these plug-ins to help you with the optimization of your content on your website.

Among the top 3 most popular ones, not ranked in hireachy are:

1) Wordpress SEO by Yoast
   This theme is easy to use as it allows you to add SEO title, meta description, and meta keywords to each post and page of your site.

   You can also write custom title for your main site, archives, category and tag pages. It also adds Open Graph meta data, Twitter Cards, Sitemaps and ping search engines whenever you update your site.

2) All in One SEO Pack
   Use All in One SEO Pack to optimize your WordPress site for SEO. It's easy and works out of the box for beginners, and has advanced features for developers or advanced users.

3) Google XML Sitemap
   This plugin will generate a special XML sitemap which will help search engines to better index your blog.

Copyright © SEO Online Marketing with SEO Diva Be Found On 1st Page of Google. All rights reserved

SEO Tools

There are many free SEO Tools that you can use to help you with your SEO works. The best tools are offered by google search engine, which is the search and the suggested keywords.

Free Tools

It also has free add-on when you download free Google Chrome to run as your search engine.

SEO Quake gives you a summary and brief overview of your SEO health and information, indicating in specific what needs to be done to improve your SEO for your website. It also gives you the ranking of your website on Alexa for your position of your website and SEMRush for your traffic.

Google Analytics also helps you track the traffic and behaviour of your customers online.

Google Webmaster gives you details of what you need to do or follow up to improve on your overall SEO for your website.

For beginner, do not confuse yourself with too many unnecessary metrics and statistics.
Simply follow the 3 basic SEO Rules of Keywords, Content and Backlinks!

SEM or Search Engine Marketing

SEM are paid advertising that you carry out through search engine like Google Adwords, Google Adword Express, Yahoo, Bing and many more.

SEM is a faster method for business owners to rank their business on search engine. However, paid advertisement can be very expensive as it is a short term solution and business owner or marketer pay for every click that is being made onto the site, whether or not a conversion or lead is generated through the advertisement.

Google Adword Paid Method

For example "best selling ebook" is super competitive and average search per month for this keyword is about 480/month while each click costs about US$1.18/click.

The keyword "SEO Book" is even more competitive and the average search per month is about 2,400/month and each click cost about US$1.57

SEO Awesome Ranking Your Online Business

What is SEO Awesome Ranking?

This is the ultimate method that would help you rank your business on the first page of google and youtube.

Using your own Youtube Channel and Youtube Marketing Video, you can now rank your business on Google and Youtube.

Copyright © SEO Online Marketing with SEO Diva Be Found On 1st Page of Google. All rights reserved

3 SEO Basic Elements Rules for Youtube Channel & Videos

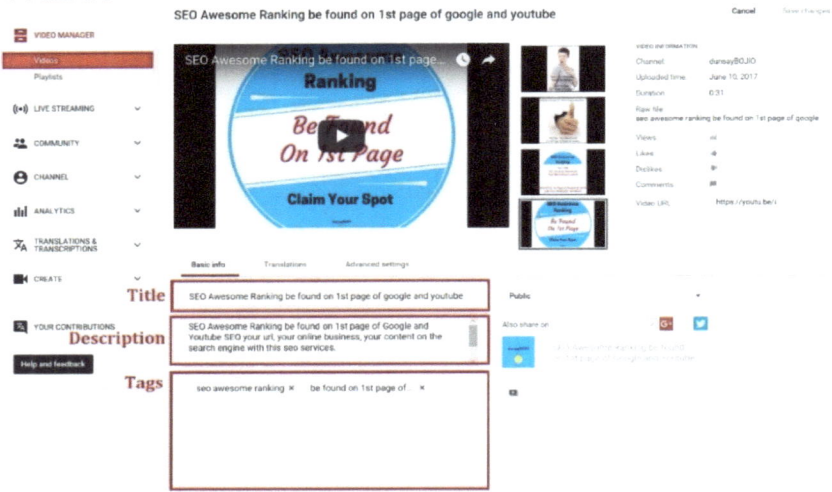

1) **Youtube Channel**
    a. Keywords
    b. Keywords Placement on Content of Your Description, Title & Media
    c. Backlinks to Website
2) **Youtube Video**
    a. Video Title
    b. Video Description
    c. Video Tags
    d. Backlinks to Website on Description
    e. Keywords Placement on Title & Description
3) **SEO Backlinks** from your youtube video to your site helps increase the quality of your SEO Website. It is lso important to create backlinks to all the other social media platforms indicated by Youtube

Copyright © SEO Online Marketing with SEO Diva Be Found On 1st Page of Google. All rights reserved

Social Media Platforms

Other than your website or youtube, your business should also establish its presence on social media platforms like facebook, Instagram, twitter and others.

SEO Social Media Platforms

The same 3 Basic Elements Rule Applies, Your Keywords, Content and Backlinks.

Compelling Content for Conversion

Yes, SEO can be costly if your content cannot convert.

It is important to brand and design compelling content for your audience. With SEO, Customers can find you online when they search for your products and services.

With Compelling Content. they would want to know more about your products and services, or buy from you online.

Call To Action For Leads or Conversion

Hence, it is important for you to build your content online with simple call to action for your online customers.

Branding and Conversion

Other than SEO, branding and conversion are also vital part of your online business.

Your content must be able to communicate WHY customers should be building the relationship or buying from you instead of your competitors.

For compelling content for your online business, connect with us at http://dunsayBOJIO.com for specific marketing strategies for your business.

Thank You

Special Thanks to:

Albert Tee
Ivan Chua
Alan Chin
Jonathan Yap
Darren Lim
Norvin
Deng Jun
Darryl Ang
Rick Choo
Shaw Tang
Kevin Ban
Alvin Peh
i-Success Mastermind Team
My loving and supportive family
All SEO Seekers and Practitioners

Back Cover

Many businesses spend about 80% of their online marketing budgets on SEO. Cut down your SEO spending when you know what you need to rank your business online.

BE FOUND ON FIRST PAGE OF GOOGLE AND YOUTUBE! Focus on your business, optimize on your SEO budget.

A book that covers what you need to know about SEO and how you too CAN RANK YOUR BUSINESS ON GOOGLE and YOUTUBE using the SEO information shared here.

Be CONSISTENT and RELEVANT to your topic to RANK!

With the information provided in this book, you DO NOT need to be TECH SAVVY to be able to DOMINATE YOUR NICHE online.

So, pick me up, read, learn and apply SEO for your online business today.

Copyright © SEO Online Marketing with SEO Diva Be Found On 1st Page of Google. All rights reserved

About The Author

Judy Toh also known as **online SEO Diva**, is a non-techy SEO Specialist with **NO coding or technical background**, who helps businesses rank on first page of Google and Youtube with SEO Awesome Ranking Technique.

SEO Awesome Ranking Technique enables her to rank targeted long tail keywords within minutes. Be shocked with the pleasant surprises of the best, fastest and easiest search engine optimization method that can elevate the quality of your SEO for your online business today.

SEO Diva started her internet marketing journey through courses and online learning. **Having found a supportive and sharing community of online marketers**, entrepreneurs and business owners has helped her to grasps strong understanding of SEO and its impact on online businesses.

Copyright © SEO Online Marketing with SEO Diva Be Found On 1st Page of Google. All rights reserved

www.ingramcontent.com/pod-product-compliance
Lightning Source LLC
Chambersburg PA
CBHW041210180526
45172CB00006B/1227